MW01131919

better together*

*This book is best read together, grownup and kid.

akidsbookabout.com

a kids book about™

a kids book about™

IDENTITY

by Taboo

a kids book about™

Text and design copyright © 2021
by A Kids Book About, Inc.

Copyright is good! It ensures that work like this can exist,
and more work in the future can be created.

All rights reserved. No part of this publication may be
reproduced, distributed, or transmitted in any form or
by any means, including photocopying, recording, other
electronic or mechanical methods, without the prior
written permission of the publisher, except in the case of
brief quotations embodied in critical reviews and certain
other noncommercial uses permitted by copyright law.
For permission requests, write to the publisher.

Printed in the United States of America.

A Kids Book About books are available online:
www.akidsbookabout.com

To share your stories, ask questions, or inquire about bulk
purchases (schools, libraries, and nonprofits), please use
the following email address:

hello@akidsbookabout.com

ISBN: 978-1-953955-06-7

Designed by Rick DeLucco
Edited by Jennifer Goldstein

This book is dedicated to my kids:
Josh, Jalen, Journey, and Jett Gomez.

Intro

Who are you? Who am I? A lot of the time, when we hear this, we simply answer with our names, but we're so much more than that! When you describe yourself to others or think about who you are, the words collect into descriptions that form what we call our identity.

But no matter how empowering discovering who we are is, it's important to remember that our identities describe us but don't define us. Some identities we are born with and some we choose, but we're the ones that give them power and meaning.

This is a book about my journey in discovering and learning about who I am and why I'm in this beautiful world. The funny thing is, it's always changing as we live each day. I hope this book helps you learn how to recognize the things that make you, you.

WHO ARE YOU?

When you hear that question,
do you answer with your name?

Or where you are from?

Or where your parents or
grandparents were born?

With what you love?

With your superpower?

You can be so many
different things.

But did you know that
any way you answer,
"Who are you?"
is part of your...

IDENTITY.

Identity is who you are, the way you think about yourself, and the things that you choose to describe yourself.

It's the combination of all the things that make you unique and special.

My name is
JIMMY GOMEZ.

But you probably
know me as **TABOO.**

My friends and
relatives call me **TAB.**

And when I'm in my zone
and ready to rock the stage...

I AM TABOO NAWASHA.

I have so many names because I'm so many things!

I'm a dancer, an MC,* and a founding member of the **BLACK EYED PEAS.**

*In hip hop culture, an MC is another way to say a rapper. I prefer to be called an MC.

But most of the time,

I'm just Jaymie's **HUSBAND.**

I'm also **DAD** to my kids.

I'm even a **COLLECTOR**
of toys and sneakers.

These are all part of my identity.

But I haven't always
been all of these things.

I grew up in **EAST LA.***

*LA stands for Los Angeles, a city in California.

I'm of **NATIVE** and **MEXICAN** descent.

My grandmother represents my **NATIVE** heritage, while my **MEXICAN** heritage comes from my grandfather.

Nanny is what we
called my grandmother.

She loved her family
and taught us the ways
of our people, which were
handed down to her.

That's part of
my identity too.

Where I grew up in California, just about everyone has **INDIGENOUS** roots, which can be traced back to Mexico.

Those roots are another part of my identity.

We are
MEXICAN AMERICAN
people and we call ourselves
CHICANOS.

Most people in East LA speak Spanglish, which is a combination of English and Spanish, and life there is a beautiful mosaic of...

MEXICAN and

AMERICAN

traditions, food, and music.

My Nanny danced to express herself, and when I dance, I feel the heartbeat and the drum of my ancestors pounding inside me.

That's part of my **IDENTITY**.

She believed in me and would set me up like a real star, calling out, "From Los Angeles, California, give it up for..."

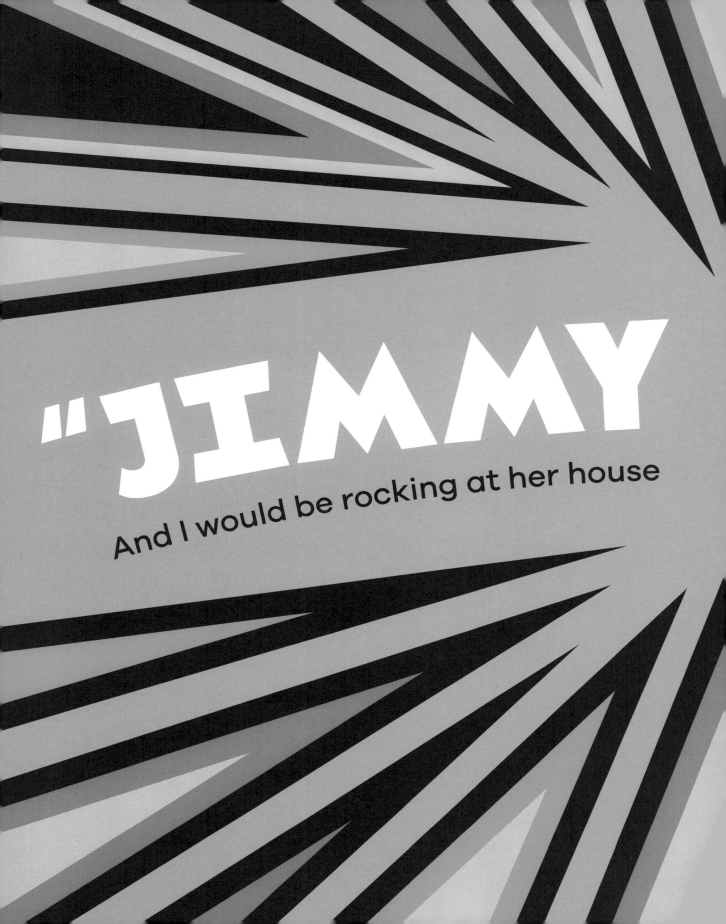

My mom's love and my grandmother's guidance were all I needed when I was younger.

I didn't grow up with my grandfather or my dad, so I learned about my **MEXICAN** heritage from the people around me.

And then my mom met a man when I was a bit older.

We eventually became a family, and a little later on, I got a brand new lil' sister.

Thanks to him, I learned
a lot about **MEXICAN** culture.

My sister's father was from Mexico
and shared amazing traditions
with us, and he even took our
family to Morelia, Michoacán,*
where he is from.

*Morelia is a city in the state of Michoacán, located in
central Mexico. It is the capital and largest city in the state!

Nanny gave me the gift of becoming a **PERFORMER** and a **DANCER**, and now that's part of my identity—who I am.

My mother's partner and the
East LA community I grew up with
showed me that sometimes,
it takes knowing someone new
to discover who you are.

Who is a person in your life
who has helped you to
discover your identity?

Identity is about who you are.

BUT NONE OF US ARE JUST ONE THING.

Some parts of our identity
we're born with.

And some of them we choose.

Parts of our identity
can be obvious to others.

And other parts might be

HIDDEN.

Others can help you along your journey to discover

WHO YOU ARE,

WHAT YOU LOVE,

and **WHAT'S TRUE ABOUT YOU.**

But you don't have to keep every name, word, or identity other people might label you with.

One of the things
I want you to know
about **YOUR** identity...

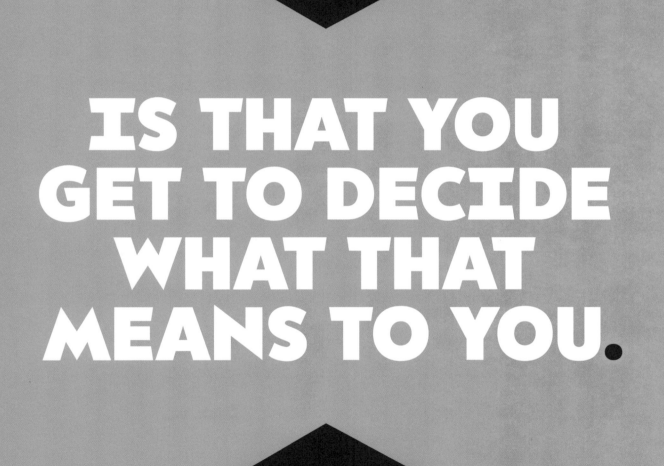

IS THAT YOU GET TO DECIDE WHAT THAT MEANS TO YOU.

Because identity is all about

BEING
WHO YO

OU ARE.

And not just that—it's also about **KNOWING** who you are.

Identity can be about your

RACE,

GENDER,

HOMETOWN,

SCHOOL,

FAITH,

or

WHAT YOU'VE LOST,

and **WHAT YOU'VE GAINED.**

As a dancer and an MC,
I get to travel around the
world and do what I love.

I get to show who I am to lots
of people and I represent my
culture with how I dress.

Identity can be things
like that too.

I like to rock a **TURQUOISE PIECE** or a lil' bit of Native bling to express my **NATIVE ROOTS** and feel like my ancestors are with me.

There's no greater
feeling than getting to be

And as you grow up, you'll keep discovering new parts of yourself.

NEW WAYS YOU IDENTIFY.

Some of them might have been there all along.

Some might start like a seed that grows over time, getting bigger as you get older.

But identity isn't just formed by **EASY** or **FUN** things—part of what shapes you is the **CHALLENGES** you've faced.

These challenges are like big,
scary giants, towering over you
trying to take you down.

I like to call it

"FIGH
GIA

TING NTS."

Because even though they may seem impossible to beat, we do have the strength to fight back and not give in to them.

Back in 2014,
I found out I had cancer.

That was one of
the biggest **GIANTS**
I ever had to **FIGHT**.

I didn't know what to do—but
my wife, kids, and family did.

Without them, I don't
think I would've had the
strength to beat it.

I knew I needed to
do everything the
doctors told me.

Their medicine worked
to stop the cancer, but it
made my body weak, and
my spirit even weaker.

During my journey of healing:

I RECONNECTED with my Native roots.

I ATE FOODS that gave my body the energy it needed.

I MEDITATED AND LISTENED to my heart.

I SPENT TIME outdoors and became one with the earth.

AND I FELT DEEP JOY to be with my family and friends who love me.

THIS CONNECTION
to my own identity helped
heal my spirit and supported
the healing of my body.

I also remembered what Nanny taught me about who I am, and that helped me get in touch with a part of me that's always been there.

Now my identity includes

being a **CANCER SURVIVOR,**

an advocate for **INDIGENOUS COMMUNITIES,**

and someone who honors **MY WHOLE SELF—**

MEXICAN and **NATIVE.**

So now that you know a bit more about me, who I am, and my identity...

WHO ARE YOU?

I AM:

_____

_____

_____

_____

_____

_____

_____

_____

Outro

Lyrics from the original song *Fighting Giants* by **Taboo**.

This is a book about identity and how I fight giants.

Yeah, let me tell you about a strong man overcoming all the things that stand in the way of what he's fighting for, but he just keeps pushing till he finds that cure for hatred, complications, those that can't see that love's the greatest thing that we all could share, if we just stand up today, we all got a voice to say!

I just want to say to you it's all right.

So, I'm gonna keep on fighting giants—no matter how big, how small, how tall—just give me one good reason I can't make them fall. You see, everything you put between us, standing outside your fortress walls, and I'm gonna keep on fighting giants till I make them fall.

Let me tell you about a world I know, where the people got so much soul, doesn't matter if you're big or small. You can be yourself if you just stand tall. Stand up! Don't you ever let 'em get you down. No turning back 'cause it's your time now. Let your sun shine bright. It will be just right today.

We all got a voice to say, I just want to say to you it's all right.

Down, down, down. Stand up!

find more kids books about

leadership, school shootings, boredom, trauma, self-love, optimism, racism, death, bullying, body image, and community.

akidsbookabout.com

share your read*

*Tell somebody, post a photo, or give this book away to share what you care about.

@akidsbookabout